BIRD WATCH

BOOK FOR KIDS

Introduction to Bird Watching, Colorful Guide to
25 Popular Backyard Birds, and Journal Pages

Contents

Let's Start Bird Watching!

BIRD WATCHING is a fun and interesting hobby that lets you enjoy nature, wild-life, and the great outdoors! You can bird watch in a wide variety of locations including your own backyard, a trail through the woods, and even a city park. Best of all you don't need any special skills or equipment to get started -- just curiosity and a willingness to get outside and observe. This guide will help you get started.

Tips for Seeing Birds

Be Quiet. Birds get startled by loud noises and will fly away and hide. Birds have very good hearing so be as silent as possible and avoid shouting when you spot a bird.

Be Patient. It can take time to spot birds. Waiting and watching for birds to appear is a big part of bird watching.

Listen Carefully. Using your ears to listen for bird calls and songs is as large a part of bird watching as using your eyes.

Stand Still. If you see a bird don't wave your hands or move quickly toward it because movement can also startle birds. It is best to move slowly and be as still as possible while waiting to spot birds.

Wear Dark Clothes. Try to wear clothing that blends in with the natural surroundings such as tans, browns, and greens. Bright and light cloth-ing such as white, yellow, or red will make you stand out and cause birds to take cover.

Be Aware of Your Surroundings. Certain birds favor specific habitats so being aware of your surroundings will help you to know which birds to look out for.

Go Early. Birds are early risers and tend to be more active in the morn-ing. In the middle part of the day many birds rest in shady spots and then become more active again in the late afternoon.

Useful Items for Birdwatching

It's time for a birdwatching adventure! Below are some useful things to bring along when looking for birds.

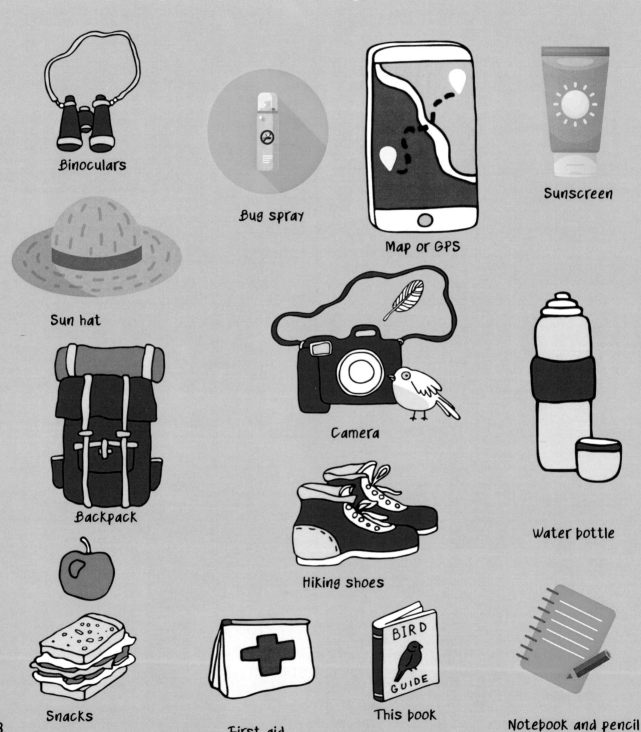

Binoculars

Bug spray

Map or GPS

Sunscreen

Sun hat

Camera

Backpack

Water bottle

Hiking shoes

Snacks

First aid

This book

Notebook and pencil

All About Birds

What makes a bird a bird?

- Birds have feathers
- Birds have wings
- Birds lay eggs
- Birds are warm blooded

Fun Facts about Birds

- Birds have been around for millions of years and evolved from dinosaurs

- There are more than 10,000 different species of birds in the world and more than 900 in North America

- Birds have hollow bones which help them to fly

- Some birds can't fly

- Many types of birds migrate, some for thousands of miles

Parts of Birds

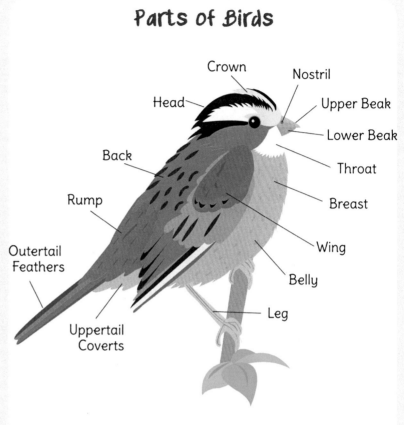

Bird Shapes

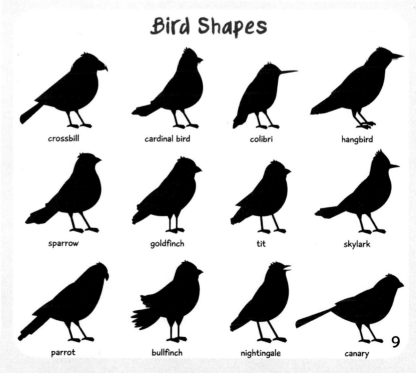

crossbill   cardinal bird   colibri   hangbird

sparrow   goldfinch   tit   skylark

parrot   bullfinch   nightingale   canary

American Crow

Appearance:

Large, all black, slightly glossy plumage; long and thick bill; squared tail feathers

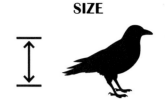

16-21 inches (40-53 cm)

Habitat:

Can be found all over the United States and Canada; habitats range from open woodlands to human inhabited areas such as city parks

RANGE

Nesting:

Both parents build nest; nests hidden in trees; 3-9 eggs; 1-2 broods per year; 16-18 days incubation; both parents care for hatchlings; young leave nest 25-35 days after hatching

Diet:

Omnivores; ground foragers; wide diet including insects, worms, seeds, fruit, garbage, carrion

Migration:

Do not migrate in winter

Conservation Status:

Low concern

Notes:

Very social, forming large flocks. Smart and inquisitive. Known for loud cawing calls.

American Goldfinch

Female

Male

Appearance:

Small birds with short, cone-shaped bills and short notched tails; breeding males are bright yellow with black foreheads and wings with white markings; females are a duller yellow with olive-green markings; nonbreeding males are light brown with faded black wings and cap

4.3-5.1 in (11-13 cm)

Habitat:

Can be found all over the United States and parts of Canada; live in open woodlands and weedy fields; human inhabited areas such as suburbs and parks

RANGE

Nesting:

Nests mid- to late summer; female builds nest in tree or bush; 4-6 eggs; two-week incubation; both parents care for nestlings; young leave nest at 10-16 days old

Diet:

Foliage gleaner; eats seeds

Migration:

Short-distance migration in winter

Conservation Status:

Low concern

Notes:

Very social, gather in flocks

13

American Robin

Appearance:

Both male and female robins are dark gray or brown on top and wings with red-orange chest; females are slightly duller in color than males

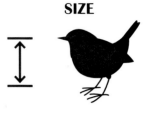

8-11.0 in (20-28 cm)

Habitat:

Can be found all over United States and Canada and parts of Mexico; lives in open woodland and fields; alco common in backyards and gardens

RANGE

Nesting:

Mate from early spring through mid-summer, 2-3 broods per year; female builds nest in tree or bush; 2-5 eggs; two-week incubation; male and female take care of hatchlings; leave nest after two weeks

Diet:

Omnivores; ground foragers; eat a variety of foods including insects, worms, berries

Migration:

Migrates south in winter; some stay put in winter depending on conditions

Conservation Status:

Low concern

Notes:

Frequent singers with clear, musical whistles

I SAW IT!

Baltimore Oriole

Male

Female

Appearance:

Medium sized with a pointed bill; males are bright orange with black heads, backs, wings, and tails; females are a duller brownish to yellowish in color

Habitat:

Found in eastern through central United States and parts of southern Canada; lives in open woodlands, edges of forests, along rivers, as well as human areas such as parks and backyards

Nesting:

Female builds nest in shape of hanging basket; 4-6 eggs; 11-14 day incubation; both parents care for hatchlings; leave nest after two weeks

Diet:

Omnivores; foliage gleaner; diet consists of insects, berries, fruit, nectar

Migration:

Migrates south in winter to Florida, Mexico, Central America

Conservation Status:

Low concern

Notes:

Distinctive whistling song; sometimes feeds by "gaping" – stabbing fruit with closed bill and then opening mouth to drink juice

SIZE

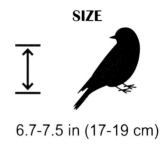

6.7-7.5 in (17-19 cm)

RANGE

I SAW IT!

Black-Capped Chickadee

Appearance:

Small body with large round head; both males and females are gray on top, wings, and tail with white underside and black cap on head and throat

Habitat:

Found in Alaska, mid- to southern Canada, and upper two-thirds of United States; lives in forest areas, open woods, and parks

Nesting:

Nest in rotting trees stumps or abandoned woodpecker holes; 5-9 eggs; 1 brood per year; two-week incubation; both parents care for hatchlings; leave nest after 14-18 days

Diet:

Omnivores; foliage gleaner; diet consists mostly of insects and spiders; also eats seeds and berries

Migration:

Do not migrate in winter

Conservation Status:

Low concern

Notes:

Mating pairs stay together for several years; form small flocks; territorial

SIZE

4.7-6 in (12-15 cm)

RANGE

Blue Jay

Appearance:

Bright blue on top with a whitish gray underside; black around neck; black and white accents in wings and tail; prominent crest on head

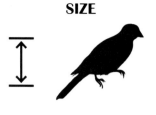

SIZE

9.8-11.8 in (25-30 cm)

Habitat:

Can be found in southern Canada and east of Rocky Mountains in United States; lives in deciduous forests and frequently seen in human inhabited areas

RANGE

Nesting:

Both male and female build nest in trees and bushes; 3-6 eggs; 1 brood per year; 17 day incubation; both pa help care for hatchlings; leave nest after 17-21 days

Diet:

Omnivores; ground forager; eat nuts, especially acorns, as well as seeds, insects, fruits, grains; store food for later

Migration:

Short-distance migration; may migrate south in winter but many do not

Conservation Status:

Low concern

Notes:

Intelligent and social bird; territorial and can be aggressive; very vocal with distinctive calls

Carolina Wren

Appearance:

Long, thin bill; small, rounded body with long tail; reddish brown upper with lighter tan underside; white stripes above eyes and white under beak; black and white accents on tail and wings

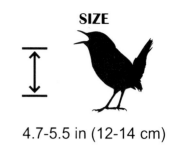

4.7-5.5 in (12-14 cm)

Habitat:

RANGE

Can be found in United States east of the Rocky Mountains and parts of Mexico; lives in open woodlands, forest edges, and suburban areas

Nesting:

Both male and female build nest; open cavities above ground; 3-7 eggs; 1-3 broods per year; 12-15 day incubation; both parents care for hatchlings; leave nest after 10-16 days

Diet:

Ground foragers; feed on insects and spiders, occasional fruit or seeds

Migration:

Do not migrate in winter

Conservation Status:

Low concern

Notes:

Live in pairs year-round; sing in duets

23

Chipping Sparrow

Appearance:

Slender with a long tail; brown with darker streaks on top, lighter gray underneath; rust-colored on top of head with black stripe through eye area

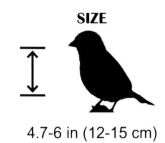

4.7-6 in (12-15 cm)

Habitat:

Found throughout North America; live in a variety of habitats including open woodlands, forest edges, fields, marshes, parks, and backyards

RANGE

Nesting:

Females built nests in trees or shrubs; 2-7 eggs; 1-3 broods per year; 10-15 day incubation; hatchlings leave nest after 9-12 days

Diet:

Ground forager; eat mostly seeds and grasses but also insects, berries

Migration:

Northern sparrows migrate south in winter

Conservation Status:

Low concern

Notes:

Form small flocks; loud, trilling song

25

Common Grackle

Appearance:

Large with long tail and long tapered bill; males are black with blue iridescent heads and a bronze sheen on body; females are smaller and lack the iridescence of the male

11.0-13.4 in (28-34 cm)

Habitat:

Found across southern Canada and in United States east of Rocky Mountains; live in open woodlands, forest edges, grasslands, meadows, marshes and near human habitation including parks, agricultural fields, suburbs

RANGE

Nesting:

Female builds nest high in tree; 2-6 eggs; 1-2 broods per year; 12-14 days incubation; both parents care for nestlings; hatchlings leave nest after 15-17 days

Diet:

Omnivores; ground forager; eat seeds, grains, insects, fruits, small animals, garbage

Migration:

Stay year-round in majority of range; northern birds will migrate south

Conservation Status:

Low concern

Notes:

Social and noisy birds; form large flocks

Downy Woodpecker

Male

Female

Appearance:

Smallest of the woodpeckers with a short bill; white chest and back, black wings with white spots, black tail and head, white above bill and eyes; males have a red patch on back of head

Habitat:

Found across United States and most of Canada; live in a variety of habitats including deciduous forests, river edges, parks, orchards, and suburbs

Nesting:

Both male and female make nest by pecking hole in dead tree; 3-6 eggs; 1-2 broods per year; 12 days incubation; both parents care for young; hatchling leave nest at 20-25 days

Diet:

Bark forager; eat insects of all types; some seeds and berries

Migration:

Do not migrate in winter

Conservation Status:

Low concern

Notes:

Form mixed-species flocks in winter

SIZE

5.5-6.7 in (14-17 cm)

RANGE

Eastern Bluebird

Male

Female

Appearance:

Small with round head and big belly; males are a vibrant blue on top with reddish brown-colored chest and throat; females are grayish brown on top with tinged blue tail and wings and paler orange-brown chest

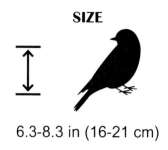

6.3-8.3 in (16-21 cm)

Habitat:

Found across southern Canada and east of the Rockies in the United States down into Mexico; live in grasslands; pastures; agricultural fields, parks, backyards

RANGE

Nesting:

Nests in cavity such as tree hollow; old woodpecker hole, or birdhouse; 3-6 eggs; 2-3 broods per year; 13-16 day incubation; both parents care for nestlings; young leave 18-20 days after hatching

Diet:

Ground forager; eat mostly insects; also berries and other fruits

Migration:

Northern populations migrate south in winter

Conservation Status:

Low concern

Notes:

Social birds that form flocks; pairs bond for several seasons

European Starling

Appearance:

Dark with iridescent feathers tinged with purples and greens, short tale and long pointed yellow bill

Habitat:

Found all over North America up into parts of Alaska and down into Mexico; tend to live near human populations in towns and urban areas; grassy areas

Nesting:

Cavity nesters including buildings, nest boxes, old woodpecker holes; males build nest; 3-6 eggs; 1-2 broods per year; 12-day incubation; young leave nest after about 21 days

Diet:

Ground foragers; opportunistic eaters but preference is insects of all types including beetles, caterpillars, and flies; berries and other fruits; grains, seeds, and garbage

Migration:

Short-distance migration; northern populations travel south in winter

Conservation Status:

Low concern

Notes:

Brought to North America in 1890 and considered by some to be a pest species; intelligent and adaptable; able to mimic the songs of other birds

SIZE

7.9-9.1 in (20-23 cm)

RANGE

I SAW IT!

Hairy Woodpecker

Male

Female

Appearance:

Almost identical to the downy woodpecker except in size and with a long straight bill; white chest and back, black wings with white spots, black tail and head, white above bill and eyes; males have a red patch on back of head and females do not

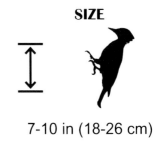

7-10 in (18-26 cm)

Habitat:

Found throughout Canada, United States, and into Mexico and Central America; live in deciduous forests; can also be found in forest edges, open woodlands, suburbs, and parks

RANGE

Nesting:

Cavity nester; excavate dead trees; 3-6 eggs; 1 brood per year; 12-day incubation; both parents care for hatchlings; youth leave nest 28-30 days after hatching

Diet:

Bark foragers; eat mostly insects with some fruit and seeds

Migration:

Majority do not migrate

Conservation Status:

Low concern

Notes:

Common and widespread birds with population increasing over the last 50 years

House Finch

Female

Male

Appearance:

Small with notched tail and conical bill; males are red around head and chest with brown back, tail, and underside accented with white; females do not have red coloring

Habitat:

Found across United States and into Mexico; live in suburban and urban areas as well as semi-open areas, farms, forest edges, and streams

Nesting:

Build nest in trees or manmade structures 12-15 feet above ground; 3-6 eggs; 3 broods per year; 13-14 day incubation; both parents care for hatchlings; young leave nest after 12-16 days

Diet:

Ground foragers; eat mostly seeds, some fruit

Migration:

Do not migrate in winter

Conservation Status:

Low concern

Notes:

Originally native to the Southwest they are now common across the United States; highly social; form large flocks

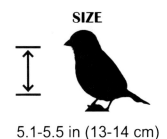

SIZE

5.1-5.5 in (13-14 cm)

RANGE

I SAW IT!

House Sparrow

Male

Female

Appearance:

Round breasted with a compact round head and short conical beak; males have reddish brown markings on head and back with gray crown and underparts and a black bib; females are shades of brown all over with a lighter grayish underside

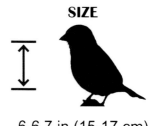

6-6.7 in (15-17 cm)

Habitat:

Found all over southern Canada, United States, and Mexico; live near people in cities, towns, and farms

Nesting:

Build nests in buildings and other human created environments, nest boxes, occasionally tree holes; 3-6 eggs; 10-14 day incubation; both parents care for hatchlings; youth leave nest 12-14 days after hatching

Diet:

Omnivores; ground foragers; eat seeds and grains, some insects and human garbage

Migration:

Do not migrate in winter

Conservation Status:

Low concern

Notes:

Since being introduced to North American in 1851, the house sparrow has flourished near humans, often outcompeting native species

House Wren

Singing

Young Wrens

Appearance:

Small, brown bird with plump body, short tail, and thin bill. Darker coloring on wings and tale, paler throat

Habitat:

Found across southern Canada, the United States, Mexico, and into South America; live in a variety of habitats including forests, swamps, thickets, and human-inhabited areas such as suburban backyards and parks

Nesting:

Cavity nesters who utilize old woodpecker holes, hollows in trees, and next boxes; 5-8 eggs; 2 broods per year; 12-15 day incubation; both parents care for nestlings; young leave nest 14-18 days after hatching

Diet:

Foliage gleaners; eats all types of insects and spiders

Migration:

Migrate south for winter

Conservation Status:

Low concern

Notes:

Small yet fierce competitors for nesting spaces, often going against much larger birds

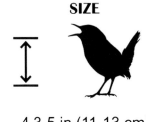

SIZE

4.3-5 in (11-13 cm)

RANGE

Mourning Dove

Appearance:

Plump body with small head and long thin tail; tan to gray with black spots on wings and and lighter on underside

9-13.4 in (23-34 cm)

Habitat:

Found across southern Canada, the United States, and Mexico; live in open woodlands, grasslands, farms, backyards, and other human-inhabited areas

RANGE

Nesting:

Tree nesters, sometimes build nest on ground; female builds nest with help from male; 2 eggs; 1-6 broods per year; 14 day incubation; both parents care for nestlings; youth leave nest 12-15 days after hatching

Diet:

Ground foragers; feed mainly on seeds, occasional berries and grasses

Migration:

Northern birds migrate south for winter, sometimes thousands of miles

Conservation Status:

Low concern

Notes:

Known for the soft, cooing sound they make; often hunted

I SAW IT!

Northern Cardinal

Male

Female

Appearance:

Large songbird with prominent crest, long tail, and short, thick bill. Males are a vibrant red with black around face and throat; females are a light brown with red accents on wings, tail, crest, and chest

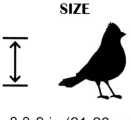

8.3-9 in (21-23 cm)

Habitat:

Found east of the Great Plains from southeastern Canada into the Southwest; lives in open woodlands, forest edges, fields, and backyards

RANGE

Nesting:

Female builds nest in foliage of trees and shrubs; 2-5 eggs; 1-3 broods per year; 11-13 day incubation; both parents care for hatchlings; youth leave nest 10-11 days after hatching

Diet:

Ground foragers; eat mainly seeds and fruit, some insects and spiders

Migration:

Do not migrate in winter

Conservation Status:

Low concern

Notes:

Territorial, males use song to defend territory and will attack intruders

Red-Bellied Woodpecker

Female

Male

Appearance:

Sleek, medium-sized woodpecker with rounded head; light-colored with black and white striped wings; males have a bright red crown and nape, females do not have red crown

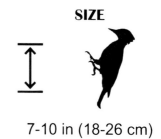

7-10 in (18-26 cm)

Habitat:

Found across the eastern United States, more common in southern states but expanding north; live in forests, woodlands, and suburbs

RANGE

Nesting:

Cavity nesters, excavates dead trees and branches; 3-6 eggs; 1-3 broods per year; 12-14 day incubation; both parents care for hatchlings; young leave nest 22-25 days after hatching

Diet:

Bark forager; eats mainly insects and spiders, supplements with seeds, nuts, fruits

Migration:

Do not migrate in winter

Conservation Status:

Low concern

Notes:

Smart and adaptable, red-bellied woodpeckers have adapted to human habitation and continue to expand their range

Red-Winged Blackbird

Female

Male

Appearance:

Medium-sized songbird with conical bill; males are glossy black with bright red spots on the top of each wing with a yellow stripe below; females are brown streaked with lighter tan

Habitat:

Widespread across North America, from Canada into Mexico; live in marshes, swamps, meadows, open fields, pastures, and water edges

Nesting:

Females build nests near the ground in brush and dense grassy areas; 2-4 eggs; 1-2 broods per year; 10-12 day incubation; both parents care for hatchlings; young leave nest 12-14 days after hatching

Diet:

Omnivores; ground foragers; wide diet including insects, worms, seeds, fruit, garbage, carrion

Migration:

Northern birds migrate south in winter

Conservation Status:

Low concern

Notes:

Aggressively defend territory; will attack larger birds; form large flocks

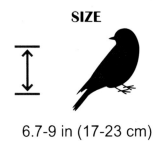

SIZE

6.7-9 in (17-23 cm)

RANGE

I SAW IT!

49

Ruby-Throated Hummingbird

Male

Female

Appearance:

Small with short, fast-beating wings and a long slender bill; bright golden green with lighter white-gray underside; males have a bright iridescent red throat

6-8 inches (15-20 cm)

Habitat:

Found east of the Great Plains from southern Canada to the Gulf Coast; live in open woodlands, meadows, fields, stream edges, orchards, and backyards

RANGE

Nesting:

Females build nests in trees or shrubs, 10-20 feet above ground; 1-3 eggs; 1-2 broods per year; 12-14 day incubation period; female cares for hatchlings; young leave nest 18-22 days after hatching

Diet:

Hovering feeders; eat the nectar of flowers, small insects and spiders

Migration:

Migrate south in winter to Central America

Conservation Status:

Low concern

Notes:

Make trip across Gulf of Mexico in single flight; attracted to backyard flowers and hummingbird feeders

I SAW IT!

Song Sparrow

Appearance:

Medium-sized, plump with round head and long tail; light grayish-brown streaked with darker shades of reddish-brown, lighter on underside

Habitat:

Found all over Canada and United States and into northern Mexico; live in a wide variety of habitats including open woodlands, marshes, grasslands, prairies, farmlands, water edges, and suburbs

Nesting:

Female builds nest close to ground in shrubs or thick grass; 3-5 eggs; 2-3 broods per year; 12-15 day incubation; both parents care for hatchlings; young leave nest 19-22 days after hatching

Diet:

Ground forager; eats mainly insects and spiders, also seeds, grains, and fruits

Migration:

Northern birds migrate south in winter

Conservation Status:

Low concern

Notes:

Abundant and widespread across North America; coloration differs depending on location; male sings to attract mates and defend territory

SIZE

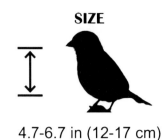

4.7-6.7 in (12-17 cm)

RANGE

Tufted Titmouse

Female

Male

Appearance:

Small and plump with thick necks and a prominent crest; gray on top and white underneath with orange shading under each wing, black spot above bill

5.5-6.3 in (14-16 cm)

Habitat:

Found east of the Great Plains in United States from Southern Maine to Florida, range has been expanding northward; live in deciduous and mixed forests, orchards, parks, and suburbs

RANGE

Nesting:

Cavity nester, build nest in tree holes, old woodpecker holes, or nest boxes; 3-6 eggs; 1 brood per year; 12-14 day incubation; both parents care for hatchlings; young leave nest 14-16 days after hatching

Diet:

Foliage gleaner; eats mainly insects and spiders, also seeds, berries, nuts

Migration:

Do not migrate in winter

Conservation Status:

Low concern

Notes:

Pairs stay together all year; often one juvenile will remain with parents and act as "helper" for next brood

White-Breasted Nuthatch

Appearance:

Small and compact with short tails and neck; gray on top with black caps and accents on wings, white on face and underside, orange-red spots on both sides near tail; females caps are more gray than black

5.1-5.5 in (13-14 cm)

Habitat:

Found in parts of Canada and across United States except for extreme south and into Mexico; live in deciduous and mixed forests, woodlands, river edges, parks, and suburbs

RANGE

Nesting:

Cavity nester, females build nests in tree holes, abandoned woodpeckers holes, and nest boxes; 5-9 eggs; 1 brood per year; 12-14 day incubation; both parents care for hatchlings; young leave nest 15-26 days after hatching

Diet:

Bark forager; eat mainly insects and spiders, also seeds and nuts

Migration:

Do not migrate in winter

Conservation Status:

Low concern

Notes:

Territorial; pairs stay together all year; loud calls

Yellow-Rumped Warbler

Female

Male

Appearance:

Full bodied with long tails; males are gray with dark streaks and white accents, bright yellow under bill, under wings, and rump; females are more brown in color

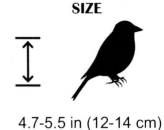

4.7-5.5 in (12-14 cm)

Habitat:

Found across North America from Alaska to southern Mexico; live in evergreen forests as well as woodland areas, near stream, parks, and suburban areas

RANGE

Nesting:

Female builds nest in tree; 3-6 eggs; 1-2 broods per year; 12-13 day incubation; both parents care for hatchlings; young leave nest 10-14 days after hatching

Diet:

Foliage gleaner; eat mainly insects and spiders, also fruits and seeds

Migration:

Far northern birds migrate south; many stay year round

Conservation Status:

Low concern

Notes:

One of most common warblers; form large flocks

BIRD WATCHING Journal

Bird Name: _____

Location: _____

When: _____

Field Notes: _____

_____

_____

Bird Name: _____

Location: _____

When: _____

Field Notes: _____

_____

_____

BIRD WATCHING Journal

Bird Name: _____

Location: _____

When: _____

Field Notes: _____

_____

_____

Bird Name: _____

Location: _____

When: _____

Field Notes: _____

_____

_____

BIRD
WATCHING Journal

Bird Name: _____

Location: _____

When: _____

Field Notes: _____

_____

_____

Bird Name: _____

Location: _____

When: _____

Field Notes: _____

_____

_____

BIRD
WATCHING
Journal

Bird Name: _____

Location: _____

When: _____

Field Notes: _____

_____

_____

Bird Name: _____

Location: _____

When: _____

Field Notes: _____

_____

_____

BIRD
WATCHING
Journal

Bird Name: _____

Location: _____

When: _____

Field Notes: _____

_____

_____

_____

Bird Name: _____

Location: _____

When: _____

Field Notes: _____

_____

_____

_____

BIRD

WATCHING

Journal

Bird Name: _____

Location: _____

When: _____

Field Notes: _____

_____

_____

Bird Name: _____

Location: _____

When: _____

Field Notes: _____

_____

_____

Made in United States
North Haven, CT
18 December 2022

29556242R00038